The Problem is YOU:
How to Get Out of Your Own Way and Conquer Self-Defeating Behavior

JOHN BURKE

The Problem is You: How to Get Out of Your Own Way and Conquer Self-Defeating Behavior
John Burke

Copyright © 2012 by Empowerment Nation

www.EmpowermentNation.com

TABLE OF CONTENTS

Introduction

"I feel like I'm trapped in a revolving door." "Nothing I've ever done has felt successful." "I am beginning to hate myself." "I'm cursed."

Millions among us suffer from depression, low self-esteem, anxiety, and addictive disorders based solely on the fact that we feel like failures. We strive for success only to feel as if there is a wall preventing us from ever taking a step forward. We face setback after setback and cannot understand how those around us seem capable of moving forward.

"Self-sabotage" is a term that refers to the act of "shooting oneself in the foot," as they say. For whatever reason or another, there are those among us who habitually prevent ourselves from fulfilling our full potential based solely on fear. Fears of failure, fears of inadequacy--even fears of success--can prevent us from moving forward, even when we believe we are making every attempt to do our best. Understanding self-sabotage means looking at our behaviors and the fears that lie beneath them. Overcoming self-destructive behaviors means committing to opening ourselves beyond those fears.

No one has to live a life in lonely solitude, driven by the inner critics in their head. Every person has the capabilities and the strength to overcome negative thinking and habits and to live a meaningful and happy life. This book will teach you how to take responsibility over your life, your career, your family life, and the outcomes of the decisions you make every day. You will learn how to attain a positive attitude and emerge from your comfort zone in your quest to becoming the manager of your life.

Chapter 1: What is self-defeating behavior?

Your own worst enemy

Sometimes called "shooting yourself in the foot," self-defeating behavior develops when we commit to solve a problem only to realize that in the course of doing so, other problems keep surfacing. These obstacles are the result of subconscious behaviors that can also get in the way of both long-term and short-term relationships.

We might recognize self-defeating behaviors when we find ourselves doing things such as "comfort eating," even if the habit has made us overweight. Other self-sabotaging behaviors include drug addiction, alcoholism, and the most common of all – procrastination. Some people practice forms of self-injury in order to escape painful emotions. Others go shopping for expensive stuff they can hardly afford in order to forget their situation. Each of us has likely succumbed to one form of self-sabotage or another, whether we were aware of it at the time or not.

The paradox of self-sabotage is that, in most cases, people reach this self-destructive state while trying to help themselves *out* *of* a destructive behavior. This occurs when someone gets upset over something and then begins to deploy a number of self-destructive behaviors with the hope that they will numb the emotional pain they are going through. The trouble is that while the behavior may appear to numb the emotional pain for a moment, in most cases these behaviors leave behind a string of negative consequences.

While self-defeating behavior happens equally among men and women, there are specific behaviors that appear to be consistent with each gender. Men are often likely to develop behaviors that edge toward the use of alcohol, drugs, or even aggressiveness; women, on the other hand, will often display behaviors related to self-injury or eating disorders.

In most cases we don't realize that we are engaging in self-defeating behavior because often the consequences are not instant. Then, because we have failed to see the correlation between our actions and their results, we are left to blame nature for our ballooning waistlines or the national economy for our overwhelming credit card debt. In many cases, we self-sabotage because we have a wrong understanding or belief about a particular behavior.

We can therefore say that self-defeating behavior is a habitual pattern that prevents a person from performing as well as they know they should.

While it is normal to struggle with issues in life, feel defeated, and regret that an expected outcome never came to be, it becomes a problem when this progression becomes the norm. When negative and defeating thoughts recur frequently, they can prevent an individual from realizing his goals.

Recognizing people driven by self-sabotage (including ourselves) may not be too easy, but with a little observation we can begin to spot people with some of the initial tendencies toward self-defeating behavior. Some of the most common forms of self-sabotage include always blaming other people, procrastination, trying to please everyone, always seeking to be right, and always having an excuse for failing to complete an assignment. Others include an obsession with perfection, taking things out of proportion, keeping grudges, playing the victim, and displaying a lack of willingness to make changes which are beneficial to oneself.

The paradox of self-defeating behavior

There are many things that could cause self-sabotaging behaviors, but in most cases they show up when things don't turn out according to expectations. A person sets out doing something with the expectation of a particular outcome, and after they have employed all of their efforts, there are no results to write home about. This is normally the point where a person is likely to self-sabotage. People with this type of behavior end up forgetting their original intent, and they spend their energy analyzing the feelings they have as a result of failing to achieve their original goal.

When this has taken place, a person begins descending in a downward spiral that makes self-sabotage a vicious cycle. Such people magnify the undesirable things in their lives to such an extent that it prevents them from accomplishing what they should in order to rectify the situation and reach their goals. In the long run, a person could finally end up failing to completely achieve their dreams.

It is therefore very easy to see how self-defeating behavior starts and how it sets itself going into a downward spiral.

Expectation of outcomes

The problem of self-defeating behavior begins with a person's expectations for a specified result from a taken action. Every time we commit to any action, it is because we expect a result. We go to take a drink of water with the expected result that it will quench our thirst. We enter relationships because we believe they will fulfill us in some way. All actions are tied to their objectives—what we want to achieve.

Expecting results from actions is normal. The problem arises when we get attached to the expected outcomes in such a way that if they don't come, we begin experiencing an emotional downward spiral that leads to self-sabotage. The downward spiral normally takes about seven steps, described as follows:

We begin by expecting a particular outcome, and when these results don't come as expected:

We begin having feelings that we deserved those results because we feel that none of our efforts should be in vain. If after a month of working out and dieting, I were to gaze at the scale and find that I had actually *gained* weight, I might feel outraged. "This work was supposed to pay off! What have I been suffering for?! Where is the *justice* of nature?"

We become filled with anger and bitterness because the outcomes we felt we deserved failed to happen as expected. "I can't *believe* I've wasted my time being miserable when I could have been eating Haagen Dazs every day! To hell with dieting!"

This makes us feel like a useless, good-for-nothing failure. "I give up. Nothing I do works out right. I'll always be a fat slob."

Since we put in all the effort that we thought we should, we feel betrayed because it surely cannot be our fault. There must be something or someone to blame for what has happened, and that is why we never got the results we deserved. "Exercise and dieting are SCAMS! I don't even *believe* in exercising anymore! Dr. Oz is a complete fraud!"

We have feelings of being deflated and powerless because our efforts have not borne fruit. "I have no choice but to suffer. The world and nature are against me."

This leads to feelings of fatigue and frustration because there is no benefit to show for all our efforts, and, as a result, we give up. "Fine. I'm going to eat a pizza. No! I'm going to eat TWO pizzas! Forget the gym—I'm never going back there again!"

This leads to confusion, and then we begin trying to analyze why things happened the way they did. We begin looking for what exactly went wrong. "Maybe it was just *that diet.* Maybe if I just *stopped eating altogether,* I'd be better off…"

In this kind of scenario, we get ourselves into a trap where we are unwilling to escape our own quagmire. Because of the resulting frustrations, our minds cannot get clear enough for us to think about our original intention and so we give up; we thereby give self-sabotage its first score in our lives.

A close consideration of the emotions in play is in order so as to clearly understand how self-defeating behavior actually sets in:

A. Feeling that you deserve the expected results

It is important to realize that the mere expectation of results does not make it automatic that the results are going to happen as we expect. The main problem here is when we believe that we "should" get the results because we feel like we deserve them. The reality in life is that things could or could not happen. Expectations, therefore, are meant to be a guideline. When things don't happen as we thought they would, we are supposed to take note of that and move on to a different way of reaching the goal. In a "healthy world," we make adjustments because things did not happen; we simply have to change our strategy.

If you drank one glass of water and it failed to quench your thirst, you might realize that you were too thirsty for one glass and logically, you would end up taking an extra glass. While the best attitude should be "let's try and see," self-sabotage stagnates by saying "it should have been like I expected," and then you become stuck. A person who is self-sabotaging stops focusing on what they intended to achieve and ends up feeling bitter or angry because things did not happen as they expected.

B. Anger and bitterness set in because you didn't get what you deserved

When we fail to get the results that we hoped for after investing in particular actions, we can become trapped in emotions that prevent us from focusing on the goal. Instead, we may begin building up or venting anger. These negative emotions cause us to stop listening to any other voice that would suggest that we could still achieve what we want. In order to solve this problem, *all we need to do is focus on changing our working formula.*

Consider again the scenario of attempting unsuccessfully to lose weight: After trying everything we have heard about (such as eating better, eating less etc.), our weight goes up instead of down. We may feel like there is no need to bother anymore, and then the impact of those extra pizzas we devoured in our exasperation will take effect, setting us back even more.

Events like these can create feelings of fatalism. These impressions may begin to creep in and make us feel as though something has predestined us to become a failure, which then leads to the next step.

C. Feelings that you are a failure because you never achieved

The next unfortunate step in the process of self-sabotage is when we begin feeling that we are actually a failure because all our efforts never bore any fruit. The truth of the matter is that *failing is not and should never be a reflection of us as individuals*. Just because the results we expected never came does not change who we really are.

"Ever tried. Ever failed. No matter. Try Again. Fail again. Fail better." – Samuel Beckett

It is important to realize that *you are different from your goals and intentions* and that they don't define who you are. In most cases, people with self-defeating behavior begin looking back at the other times they have failed at other things, and this inevitably leads to feelings of depression and disillusionment. When results don't come, the best thing you can focus on is the strategy that you employed and why it failed, so that you can *change the strategy* as you move forward.

D. Someone or something else is to blame

The next step after failure is that we may decide that because we have tried everything and it did not work, then it is not our fault and there must be someone else or something else to blame. The problem with putting blame on other people or circumstances is that we deny ourselves the power to create a different set of parameters and, as a result, we cannot move an inch forward.

E. Fatigue and discouragement set in because you feel like you have tried enough

After our minds tell us that there is someone else to blame, we finally think that this is the end of our efforts and there is nothing else we can do. It may appear like the world and all circumstances have ganged up against us and our efforts. Perhaps fate has it that we are just unlucky and cannot achieve no matter what we do. This leads to giving up on our power to decide the direction our lives are going to take.

F. Feelings of powerlessness because your efforts "never" succeed

Since we are blaming other people for failing to achieve the results that we felt like we deserved, it is normally at this moment that we may cede all of our power to decide the direction of our lives. "From this point forward, I will eat 40 pounds of ice cream every day because whatever I do doesn't make any difference."

From the moment we decide that all the knowledge we had about our goal was not helpful, we take away our power to make things happen as they should. The mindset of feeling powerless ensures that we no longer expect any results from our efforts, and instead we concentrate on our frustration. We end up being powerless and cannot make any changes to our plans or circumstances because our thought process is already fixed.

So how do we break the feeling of powerlessness? By keeping our focus and determination on the goal. If a baseball player missed catching a ball and just walked off the field in frustration, he wouldn't be a baseball player for long, would he? If instead he kept his focus on the next ball that came his way, he would have a chance to improve his stats. The same applies to us. Keep your eye on the ball and not on your failures. Failure is nothing more than a learning process to lead us to the right answer.

G. Feelings of confusion

When we have reached this stage, the mind will normally start to replay the events that just took place and look for reasons why the expected outcomes were not realized. This should be the time to ask ourselves why things did not happen and what wrong turns were taken. Instead of spending our energy on what we *could have done or should have done*, our focus should be on making the correct adjustments that will help us to succeed in our goal.

Self-defeating behavior comes as a result of failing to get back to the basics when we do not reach our intended goals after all our earnest efforts. When the desired results are not achieved, we must learn to ignore the noises of self-blame and instead keep focus on our ultimate goal.

Ask yourself these simple questions:

- How did I get where I am?

- How can I achieve my goal?

- What do I need to do differently?

- What am I willing to do in order to achieve my goal?

- What do I need to change about my current situation?

- What adjustments do I need to make in my current plan?

When we have not achieved the goals we thought we deserved, this does not mean that we are a failure. The learning process of failure will place us one step closer to achieving our goals. It is important to refocus our thoughts back to the results we desired so that we can *move forward* instead of becoming trapped by self-defeat.

Chapter 2: Characteristics of self-defeating behavior

Self-defeating behavior has been defined as those deliberate things that people will do with the full knowledge that they will cause them some trouble at the end of the day. These things are normally negative, and they will have a negative impact on a person's projects. There are many theories that have been fronted by psychologists regarding this type of behavior, but when all is said and done, these are people who will somehow harm themselves even when they know that what they are doing will cause them a negative outcome.

There are about three types of self-defeating behavior models that are known to exist:

i. **Primary self-destruction**: This refers to people who deliberately hurt themselves with full knowledge that their action will definitely hurt them, but they still go on with the intended action.

ii. **The conceptual model**: This is also called the tradeoff model and involves a person making a deliberate tradeoff in a situation. A person chooses an option that they know has some small benefit but also carries some considerable risk as well. Even though they know it will definitely hurt them, because it has some benefits, they move on with their self-handicapping behavior.

iii. **Counterproductive strategies**: This includes self-defeating behaviors where a person does not necessarily desire or even foresee what harm their behavior will cause them. A person may be pursuing a desirable goal but will decide to employ strategies that are likely to backfire and give results that are completely opposite from what was expected.

While no one truly knows the reasons for self-sabotage, in many cases it occurs when we feel that our self-esteem or ego has been threatened. Sometimes our self-esteem is under threat because we have failed to achieve the results we feel we deserved, so we become very susceptible to feelings of anxiety, distress, and depression. This leads to a situation of self-regulation in relation to success that finally leads to the downward spiral of self-defeating behavior.

There are several characteristics that we display when we have self-defeating behavior. These include:

Feelings of responsibility for others

One of the leading characteristics of a person with self-defeating behavior is confusion concerning the things that a person can change and that which they cannot, especially in relation to the feelings of other people. Whether we're talking about a romantic relationship or any other type of relationship, these individuals don't realize that there are things about other people that they cannot change. The mistaken belief these people have is that it is their responsibility to make other people happy because they love or cherish them.

The truth of the matter is that there is nothing we can do in order to ensure that other people are happy in their lives. Because of this type of confusion, we may end up worried, disturbed, suffering needless guilt, in despair, or hopeless because of and on behalf of others.

While it is easier for us to be unaffected by the sadness of a person we don't have any feelings for, trouble comes when the person suffering is someone we love and value; we feel that *this person* does not deserve to suffer. Perhaps the person we are feeling for is being mistreated by their spouse or employer; we can do well to sympathize with them because we are connected.

However, when we take it upon ourselves to feel responsible for what they are going through, we develop a self-defeating pattern of behavior. The trouble with this pattern of thought is that it will only make matters worse for both parties. Instead of spending our energy in looking for a solution that could improve matters, we will spend time and energy worrying about things that we can't necessarily do anything about.

No matter how much we value a person, it should be noted that in a healthy relationship we need to be responsible TO a person instead of being responsible FOR them. Trying to live for others, whether they are our loved ones or not, will not impart any benefits to them. Sometimes, we end up making people parasites that learn the art of living off others. Such enablers end up making sure that the "aggrieved" party never gets to live as an individual but continues to live off others' emotions.

While it is important to try to assist the people we love so as to make them happy, there is no way we can replace their minds with ours or think and act on their behalf. Everyone has the prerogative for their individual happiness. A person's happiness lies in their application of any knowledge they have in order to improve their lives; they must uphold some values, purpose, reason, and self-esteem. If anyone cannot choose those values for themselves, there is no way anyone else can be responsible for their happiness.

Many people, for whatever reasons, incurred this notion in their childhood that they ought to live for others and especially those that are close to them. While we do not live solely for our own happiness, we must reject the feeling that our loved ones' happiness is our responsibility and that when they are not happy it is we who have failed. Whether it is your child, spouse, or lover, they must personally choose whether they will be happy or not.

Failure to take our own responsibility

The second characteristic of self-sabotage concerns how a person relates to failure. No one loves failure because it is normally associated with very bleak connotations. However, we need to realize that this word applies to us in almost every stage of our lives. Failure happens to everyone—whether they are religious leaders, politicians, educators, rock stars, or just about anyone else. Failure is a reality that we desperately try to avoid, but when it happens we need to remind ourselves that it is human. Most of the achievements that anyone has ever made were motivated by the drive to avoid failure. Trouble comes when we cannot accept that failure is normal, and, as such, we can never take responsibility when failure does come to us.

Learning to take responsibility for our failures means that we are mature, and there is no way we can arrive at maturity until we reach a level where we can own up to our mistakes. A good example of this problem is a student who comes late to class and blames his or her parent for not waking them up; another is when someone fails to pass a test and then blames the teacher for having never taught them well. *We are all guilty of this at some point in our lives.*

People who continually blame their failure on others and shift responsibility can be perceived as cowards. However, even cowards may admit that their failure is based on a lack of courage. Acceptance of failure and taking responsibility requires humility, honesty, and strength of character. When we deny any culpability, we also deny ourselves opportunities to learn from any mistakes we made.

The desire to please everyone

Bill Cosby once said, "I don't know the key to success, but the key to failure is trying to please everybody." This may not be the only key to failure, but there is a great deal of truth in this statement because another characteristic of self-sabotage is the desire to please. While trying to please people is not a bad thing, when it becomes a person's responsibility to try and please everyone all the time, they will end up spreading themselves too thin. People who try to please everyone by meeting all demands will find themselves on a highway that will lead them to feeling stressed out sooner rather than later. This is because it is a feat that can never be accomplished, and feelings of failure soon crop up.

The major problem of trying to please everyone is that in doing so, we will actually abandon our own ideals. We must remember that not everyone shares our ideals, ethics, and morals, and when we stoop down to accommodate everyone, we end up being unhappy ourselves. This does not mean that we should stop trying to please each other; on the contrary, we should do as much as we can to please those we can. The beginning of the problem comes when we begin measuring our success by counting how many people we were able to please or not please.

It is important to know how much we are capable of accomplishing, and that our best may not be good enough for some people. If we have done our best according to our ability, there is no reason for us to begin crucifying ourselves; we cannot control what other people think about our best effort. This should actually be their problem and not ours. Maturity is coming to terms with this fact; we must treat everyone with respect and kindness, but that does not make it our responsibility to make sure that each and every one of them is pleased.

It is a good thing to seek the happiness of others but we should not make it our personal responsibility and priority. People who self-sabotage don't realize that others have different expectations on them, some being realistic while others are not.

You may be surprised to know that if some people had their way, this is what could occur:

- Others would want you to hang around with them on a daily basis and at every moment, even though you need to be attending work or school.

- Others would love to partner with you in their projects even though you don't have the slightest interest in what they are doing.

- Your parent may want to be with you all the time even though you have your own spouse and kids who need to spend time with you.

It is very easy to have many "important" people in your life, all of whom have their different expectations of you, and as such it is simply impossible to please every one of them every time. Trying to achieve this can be maddening, and it can drive you crazy to say the least.

When we attempt to please everyone, we soon whittle ourselves away like a pencil when it is sharpened. With each and every sharpening, the pencil gets shorter and shorter until finally nothing is left of it. This can happen to us when we allow ourselves to become spent pleasing others.

Perfectionist tendencies

Perfectionism is another serious characteristic of self-sabotage because it refuses to accept anything that is considered short of perfect. The plain truth is that almost everyone has a deep desire to have things around them that exhibit the best elements of quality. However, it is possible to become obsessive with unrealistic details of perfection to such an extent that it sabotages any effort that we may be putting toward performing at our best. People with this tendency will normally place demands on themselves that are truly unrealistic.

The issue of perfectionism is a product of the mind because it analyzes and makes decisions regarding what it calls perfect. The mind is always busy categorizing, measuring, and observing everything it comes across. The thoughts that we deduce are a result of this analysis and not a product of the feelings or the heart. People with this tendency unquestioningly take everything the mind analyzes whether or not this analysis of situations is realistic.

Many people's perception of life is in black and white; if something is not right, then it is definitely wrong, and when it is not blessed, it is definitely cursed. However, in many cases we realize that our interpretation of the same situation is totally different from that of others. This is one reason that people think that perfection is impossible to obtain. Some people have the perspective that you must put forth lots of energy and effort in order to achieve; it is only then that they feel like they have accomplished something.

Sometimes we may have a mental concept of ourselves that does not match the reality of who we really are. We expect that we should feel or react in certain ways in order to portray the perfect self-image. As a result of this, we judge everything about ourselves and our reactions as being short of the perfect image. We end up erroneously judging our feelings, and we also judge ourselves harshly for having those feelings. Because of a wrong concept of ourselves, we can end up confused and even frightened of ourselves.

It is important to understand the fact that there is no way we can be perfect. Our attitudes about ourselves and the things that surround us must change so that we free ourselves from this harsh judgment that leads to self-condemnation. It is also important to know that because of our human experience, things can never be as perfect as we might like them to be. So long as we have done something to the best of our knowledge and our ability, if the results we think we deserved don't happen as they should have, we should understand that it is the norm of things on this planet. The best we can do is to learn a lesson on how to do it better next time.

When we dwell on *what should have been,* we are tying ourselves to a situation of perfectionism and we often end up hurting ourselves and other people in the process. Accepting things as they have come without condemning ourselves leads to a state of relaxation and peace while giving ourselves an opportunity to do things differently the next time.

The most important thing we must remember is that as human beings we are less than perfect, and mistakes are bound to occur at one time or another. Healthy people consider mistakes as an opportunity to learn as opposed to a form of judgment on themselves. By adopting this viewpoint, we can begin to perceive individual failures as the components of our long-term success.

Fear of commitment

Fear of making commitments is among the most common characteristics of self-defeating behavior. This type of fear reveals itself especially in romantic life because in many cases the people suffering from this problem have a deep longing for love and connection—the very thing they seem to fear the most. The paradox of this fear is what makes it a very devastating self-sabotaging behavior. When our deepest fear is making a wrong decision because wrong decisions are considered permanent, we develop scenarios of feeling trapped.

It is important to know that these fears of commitment are tied to some form of anxiety. The most important thing in dealing with fear of commitment is to try and understand the underlying factor. If this is affecting you, there are many underlying causes that include (among others):

i. **Baggage**: There could be a combination of past experiences that you have gone through that make you cautious and even fearful of committing yourself into other relationships. Perhaps you have had to deal with a cheating spouse or lover, and as a result you now fear trusting another person again. You may believe that when you trust another person you become vulnerable to getting hurt and being heartbroken again, which is quite understandable. The easiest way to deal with this kind of hurt is to constantly learn how to evaluate the person you are dealing with in relation to the people you may have dated or had relationships with before and who hurt you.

ii. **Loss of freedom**: The other reason you may become afraid of commitment is the belief that it means surrendering to the person you are committing to. You could believe that you will be tying yourself to that person and that you will never be able to get into any other romantic relationships. Some people may consider this a lack of freedom that removes any independence they may have had. There may also be the fear that you will lose privacy because you will be living with another person. If this is your fear, it is important to count the benefits of the alliance in comparison with what you stand to lose.

iii. **Childhood experiences**: It is possible that you could have been exposed to bad relationships at the home where you grew up because of issues such as cheating, physical abuse, or divorce. It is very easy for anyone who has grown up in these situations to fear that commitment will mean inviting similar situations into his or her own life. If this did occur, it is important for you to assess your current relationship with what you know happened in your childhood to see if there are any similarities. Unless there are warning signs that you are denying, in most cases it is possible to see signs of bad behavior in the early days of any relationship.

Overcoming commitment fears

The good news is that if any of these situations apply to you, you can easily deal with your fear of commitment by taking the following simple steps to help you achieve better relationships:

i. **Don't be in a hurry**: Learning to take relationships slowly until you feel like you are truly trusting of the person you are dealing with is important. Commitment in relationships is a beautiful thing because they help people grow in love and support for one another. When the focus isn't on hurrying, it helps put a fearful mind to ease and supports the healing from any unpleasant experiences that may have occurred in the past. If a possible partner really loves or cares for you, they will not mind adhering to a reasonable timetable for the sake of the relationship.

ii. **Avoid unhelpful actions**: Sometimes, fear can cause us to suddenly shut out a partner or sabotage the entire relationship out of irrational fear. If this is you, the easiest path to avoid trouble is to be honest about your feelings. By doing this, you are letting your partner know that there is anxiety that you want to overcome as an individual, and that they have done nothing wrong.

iii. **Honesty is the best policy**: Take time to talk to your partner about any fears that are gnawing at you because this allows your partner to support you as far as the relationship is concerned. There are possibilities that your new partner can help you work through your issues and that he or she will prove worthy of that trust. Honesty builds trust. As you work through your issues, take time to listen to your partner and expect that you will be listened to as well.

iv. **Seek professional help**: If you are dealing with issues that cause anxiety and fear, and you truly feel that they are getting out of control, you will be better off seeking help from a qualified person. Therapists and other professionals can improve your life by helping you to assess and deal with your past, and thus, to accurately assess your life in its current state. The ideal situation is for you to deal with your feelings, and if you realize that you can't, then the wise thing to do is to seek therapy.

Chapter 3: The origin of incorrect beliefs

Personal experiences

In all cases, the decision to indulge in self-defeating behavior is a personal one. Most people wonder how it can be possible that they can actually make deliberate decisions to harm themselves and to prevent themselves from getting what they truly desire. The plain truth is that our subconscious minds are where the problem normally lies, and our subconscious can play tricks on our conscious mind. Self-defeating behavior is normally a result of competition between the conscious and the subconscious minds where the latter is allowed to win.

Take a situation where someone comes up with an excellent business idea or is given a challenging project to do. At the onset they start bubbling with enthusiasm and begin to lay plans with total dedication toward its achievement. However, in a matter of days, the person finds himself beginning to lose the fire he had without any particular reason and the excitement simply fades away. While the conscious mind wants to carry on the project or business idea, the subconscious mind, which houses fears and past experiences, begins to send negative messages of how they tried and failed in the past.

This creates lack of faith in the person's ability, which in turn kills their morale.

Fear of success or failure: Our minds can get conditioned in a certain manner because of the past experiences we have been through. The subconscious mind will remind us about a personal friend or a close relative who succeeded and how people became hostile to him. Or, on the other hand, it may recall another who didn't succeed at the task they set out to do and was ridiculed by others. These experiences linger in our minds, and they finally become part of our subconscious mind, which then associates any success or failure with fear and pain. What can then occur is that anytime we want to do a big project the subconscious triggers self-sabotaging behavior, and we may end up giving up before we can achieve.

Sound familiar to you? Overcoming a faulty belief system will empower you and give you the strength needed to deflect self-sabotaging behavior.

Thoughts

If you allow self-defeating thoughts and feelings to occur, they will go against anything you are trying to accomplish. These thoughts always take the opposite direction from where you want to find yourself; they end up crashing your dreams and achievements so that all your desires end up becoming your enemies. There are many self-defeating thought patterns that are quite common and they include, among others:

i. **Everything or nothing**: When a situation does not turn out as expected, you may consider yourself a total failure. Try and picture someone on a slimming diet that tastes a spoonful of ice cream, and then tells themselves that they have already blown it after just that one spoonful. As a result, they end up eating a whole quart.

ii. **Overgeneralization**: A single negative event could lead you to feeling like you have been rejected totally, and you end up using words such as "never" or "always" when you think about what happened.

iii. **Negative mental filter**: A single negative event is taken out of proportion, and you dwell on it exclusively, creating "a mountain out of a molehill." Let's say you developed a presentation at work and everyone tells you that you did a great job. However, there is one negative person who criticizes your presentation. Instead of concentrating on the positive feedback, you dwell on that one negative comment and it ruins your entire day.

iv. **Denying the positive**: You decide to reject any positive experiences you have had by thinking that they don't really count. When you have done a good job, you cannot afford to pat yourself on the back because you think anyone else could have done it. This normally leads to feelings of inadequacy, and you feel unrewarded.

v. **Jumping to conclusions**: You conclude that any negative reaction is because of a lack of approval for you. You always choose the negative side of things by thinking that nothing ever turns out positively for you.

vi. **Magnifying**: You use a magnifying glass when looking at your shortcomings or problems, but you minimize any positive qualities that you may have.

vii. **You reason emotionally**: You make the wrong assumption that any negative emotions you are feeling are probably right. If you feel guilty, you imagine that it is because you are a bad person. You feel inferior and hopeless for no reason, and you end up believing that you are actually right.

viii. **Labeling**: You use big labels to describe any shortcomings. When something goes wrong, instead of simply saying you made a mistake, you call yourself a loser. You also use labels such as a failure, fool, or jerk when describing yourself. These labels unfortunately lead to feelings of anxiety, anger, low self-esteem, and frustration.

ix. **Personalizing blame**: You have the tendency to hold yourself responsible for anything that goes wrong even when it is something that is totally out of your control. As an example, if a parent is told that her child is having difficulties, she immediately believes it is because of her poor parenting abilities. On the other hand are those who do the exact opposite and blame other people. If the marriage is not working out, it is always their spouses' fault.

Habits

Some of the habits that lead to self-defeating behavior include making conscious choices to do things that don't keep our best interests at heart. Sometimes these are habits that have been learned since childhood because we were taught that it was the only way to stay safe, but many years later we still carry on blindly. Even though they could be habits that produce short-term effects, in the long run they end up costing us more.

Some of these habits that could be causing self-defeating behavior in your life include:

i. **Addiction to struggle**: Sometimes you may be used to doing things the hard way because it is the way you have always done them. Perhaps you may even feel guilty when you get the same results in an easier way.

ii. **Believing change is hard**: You may believe that changes are inconvenient and, as such, you don't create time for seeking better ways of doing things. You may know that your work would go ten times faster if you took a computer seminar, but you don't feel like you have the time or the energy to put forth the effort.

iii. **One setback and you give up**: All that is required for you to "prove" that something won't work is a single setback, and you may believe that it is not worth your effort.

iv. **Not starting on time**: Waiting until it is too late in the day before you begin something and thereafter failing to accomplish anything because there wasn't sufficient time to follow through.

v. **Exaggerating reality**: You may spend too much time worrying about what others will think about you when you make the changes that you should make, or exaggerating reality because you want to avoid feeling anger, guilt or resentment.

vi. **False hope**: Having illusions that things will change on their own without your input.

vii. **Believing negative people**: You give in to detractors even when you know that you have a clear vision that you have been keen on achieving. You put yourself and your needs last because you feel you need approval if you are going to achieve that which you need to achieve. Sometimes you may allow yourself to get intimidated by the achievements of others because you believe that they are better than you in terms of education and background.

viii. **Remaining in the past**: You believe what you have achieved or not achieved in the past is a precursor of your entire future, instead of using it as feedback for attaining a better approach.

ix. **Lack of a schedule**: You let your day begin and roll away without planning what you are going to do. Sometimes you may fill your day with trivial things that will not directly contribute to you achieving your goals or making you a better person.

How to overcome incorrect beliefs

i. **Identify and accept**: You must identify and accept the presence of self-defeating behavior in your life and that it is short-circuiting all your efforts to move on. This is an important step that helps you realize that you need help to deal with the behavior.

ii. **Take responsibility**: You must take responsibility for your successes and your failures in order to take the direction of your future into your own hands. When you understand that you are responsible for your actions, you give yourself the power to change them.

iii. **Positive self-talk**: After you have taken responsibility for your life into your hands and made plans to change, you must put those plans into action. You change your self-image by creating vivid, positive, mental images about how you are going to succeed and the pleasure you are going to experience with the success.

The incorrect beliefs that we have developed based upon our personal histories, fears of success or failure, and negative thoughts or habits, are overcome when we take responsibility for ourselves and our actions. Develop habits that build motivation. Focus your thoughts on what you want and why you want it. Assess your past without judgment, but with objectiveness and openness to change. Allow yourself to examine your fears and why they came to be. When you find yourself becoming immersed in feelings of futility, take a moment to assess where these feelings are based, and then, without judgment, let them go.

Chapter 4: How to recognize and diminish self-defeating behavior

Developing discipline to complete tasks

When it comes to recognizing people with self-defeating behaviors, you only need to observe how they perform their tasks, and you will know them. These are people who are normally very enthusiastic about beginning new tasks even before they finish the task they are working on. Such people will have hundreds of uncompleted tasks because they have what can be referred to as "undisciplined enthusiasm." While enthusiasm is a good trait, when it comes to entertaining new tasks and concepts, a great deal of discipline is required. Because these people never get to finish a project before they start another one, they may never get to see the rewards of their hard work.

If you feel this affects you as well, there are a few strategies that you can use in order to avoid the tendency of never being able to complete your tasks:

i. **Focus on tasks**: You must commit to remaining focused on a task until it is completed. It is important to focus on completion instead of having too many projects and tasks that are in uncompleted phases. Instead of employing your enthusiasm on every new project, use it to complete the task at hand before moving on.

ii. **Have definite steps**: Define the steps that are needed to complete every task before you start working on it. While there can be some twists and turns along the way, it becomes easier to complete a task when you know where you are going ahead of time.

iii. **Every phase is a project**: After you know where you are going, you must consider every phase of your task as a complete mini-project without forgetting the bigger picture. This will give every phase of the task the attention it deserves.

iv. **Eliminate distractions**: Focus all of your energy on the task at hand, and don't allow for distractions. The problem with allowing yourself to get distracted is that it takes a long time before you can get back on track.

v. **Don't get tempted by new ideas**: There are people who find new ideas irresistible; the best thing to do is to note such an idea down and to check on it only after you have completed the task at hand.

vi. **Eliminate time wasters**: Some people's lives are full of stuff that is not really connected to the task they are doing. If this is you, it is possible that you are wasting time doing things that will not help you to complete your task. Don't take up new commitments that will dissipate the energy you need in order to finish the task at hand.

vii. **Reward yourself**: In order to learn to enjoy completing tasks, once you have completed one, reward yourself. That way you will not only be a starter but can always look forward to completing tasks in anticipation of a reward.

Overcoming feelings of helplessness

While everyone feels helpless once in a while, there are those who get so helpless that it becomes too difficult for them to ever get back on track. In many cases, these feelings of helplessness take root in a person's life and affect his or her way of thinking. When care is not taken, these feelings can cause a serious disruption in their life. The longer a person feels helpless, the less they will have proper control over their lives. You can quickly recognize people with self-defeating helplessness because of the following characteristics:

- They feel that they cannot succeed in life no matter what they do. They may also easily become dependent on other people to solve even the smallest problem in their lives because they feel totally incompetent.

- They develop a deep fear that they cannot handle any situation, and they end up becoming miserable, depressed, and totally unhappy with their lives.

- They consider themselves victims who are always in need of rescue, and they have a generally pessimistic view of their entire existence because they think they are perceived as weaklings.

- They finally become despondent simply because their friends are tired of babysitting them to solve all their problems. This despondency makes them resigned to their fate since they feel they cannot change.

If this applies to you, these are ways that you can escape the trap of self-defeating helplessness:

- Begin by identifying those obstacles, fears, and challenges that make you feel completely helpless, and ask yourself why they make you feel that way. Look for ways to encourage yourself to move from depending on others, to independence. The self-confidence you acquire in this process will assist you in dealing with any such challenges in the future.

- Teach yourself ways to deal with your helplessness when it crops up and to confront conflicts and problems as soon as they arise without letting them linger on.

- Pick up your life anytime you relapse into the old lifestyle by reminding yourself that it is only normal. When you score any success, don't forget to reward yourself.

- Remind yourself that it will take time to get to freedom from helplessness, and, as a result, you must be patient with yourself during that time. Allow yourself to adjust to a new way of dealing with problems without aiming for instant perfection.

Resisting denial and recognizing other options

The mind uses denial as a coping mechanism, especially when things we don't want occur in our lives. This is a natural thing to do because we all want our lives to be in order. There is an amount of denial that is acceptable in an emotionally healthy person because they are able to focus on the positive and stay motivated in life. However, there are other forms of denial that are not at all healthy. These types of denial come into play when there are things that ought to be done, yet we choose not to do them because it will involve a level of discomfort.

Negative types of denial involve:

i. **Denying that a problem exists**: A popular form of denial is refusing to admit that there is a problem as soon as it crops up. When the problem finally becomes a giant, they wonder why they never saw it when it started. This is normally the challenge when someone ignores a problem hoping that it will solve itself.

ii. **Denying the significance of the problem**: Another problem is when a person denies the magnitude of a problem, especially when it is still small. They think everything is fine until it grows too big for them to handle. A good example is when an alcoholic begins as a social drinker thinking that they will quit when they feel like it, until it is too late.

iii. **Denying available options**: In cases like these, a person admits there is a problem and that it may be a big one that requires assistance from outside; however, they tune their minds to believe that there is no way it can be solved. As a result, they see no need of trying any form of solution.

iv. **Personal responsibility**: This involves when a person knows that they have a problem that requires a solution, but they refuse to admit their responsibility to initiate change. Such people may even say they were born that way, and, as such, they cannot change no matter what.

v. **Urgency of time**: Another form of denial is that which keeps people from dealing with the problem immediately when they notice it because they think they will have some time later to deal with it. They always think there will be a more appropriate time to deal than the present.

If you find yourself dealing with any one of these forms of denial, there are simple things you can do in order to overcome them. These include:

i. Examine and admit that there are areas in your life where you are not being at all honest with yourself. Find the thoughts that are keeping you from dealing with situations and what you are trying to avoid.

ii. Focus your energy on those things that you have been ignoring and avoiding. Find the lies that you have been telling yourself and what you can do in order to deal with these situations once and for all.

iii.   Experience and accept the truth about any situation even if the situation is an unpleasant one. It is always better to face a situation even if it brings feelings of embarrassment or depression than to deal with the consequences of denial much later.

iv.   Avoid putting off dealing with situations as they arise. It is always much easier to deal with one problem when it is still fresh than lumping several of them together until they suffocate you all at one time. Remember that disappointment and setbacks are a part of life, and when you have dealt with them you will come out stronger and feeling better.

Overcoming procrastination

There are millions of people who always feel like they are late in handing in their projects or even fulfilling their dreams. They discover that everybody else is always completing things ahead of them, yet they may have had the same amount of time and the same set of circumstances. These are, more often than not, people who wait until the last minute before they start doing a task because they believe they will have all the time in the world to perform.

Such is the curse of procrastination: at the end of the day procrastinators end up feeling guilty because procrastination halts their progress almost completely. The results of procrastination seriously affect a person's self-esteem because of how little they are able to accomplish.

How to recognize procrastination

There is no way that a person can deal with procrastination unless they understand what the underlying causes are. Sometimes they will notice that they are never prepared to start an assignment because they may not be in the right mood; they wait until a later time when they think that they will be in a better mood. Normally these are just excuses that the mind employs to cover up the self-defeating habit of procrastination. Some of the root causes of procrastination include:

i. **Apparent difficulty**: The mind of a procrastinator tells them that the assignment they are about to begin is difficult, stressful, or even boring, and that is enough to stall the process of beginning.

ii. **False security**: A person who procrastinates normally believes they have all the necessary energy, and that they will be able to begin when they want and complete the task in no time. It is possible for a few of them to marshal sufficient energy required to finish the task, but in most cases this is the exception rather than the rule.

iii. **Waiting for the right time**: People who procrastinate normally think that the ones who finish tasks on time work only when they feel like working or when they have the right mood. The truth of the matter is that those who don't procrastinate begin working whether they are in the mood or not. Sometimes they work even when they are feeling terrible, and their moods change as they work.

iv. **Fear of failure**: In most cases the reason for procrastinating is a fear of failure. This fear is such that these people are afraid of beginning a task until they are sure they will do it successfully. They are afraid of what other people will say if they begin an assignment and fail to complete it.

How to overcome procrastination

If you find that this is something that affects you and that you wish to overcome, there are simple steps you can take. Overcoming the self-sabotaging behavior of procrastination requires that you first acknowledge that it is a problem that you need to deal with, and it is not simply a bad habit. Some people end up in a deep depression because of procrastination, and, in the most severe cases, it can lead to suicidal tendencies. However, you can easily overcome procrastination by following these simple strategies:

- Keep in mind that the awaited "good mood" may never come.

- Understand that any fears you harbor have the potential to grow into giants as long as they are not dealt with on time.

- Realize that by continuing with procrastination you are setting yourself up for failure, disappointment, and perhaps depression at the end of the day.

- Know that the people who don't procrastinate never wait for the right moment before they can begin working on any project; they normally begin regardless of what their moods are, and somehow the good moods catch up with them as the project continues to unfold.

Letting go of bad habits

Sometimes people wonder why it is that everyone else appears to be moving almost effortlessly towards the top while they themselves remain stagnant in their jobs or social lives. In most cases, the reason they are stagnant is that they have an unpleasant habit they may not be willing to give up on. This may look like a small habit to them, but it may be possible that they have stayed with this habit for so long that they do not even know that it annoys their colleagues and other people in their life. While there are many of these habits, some of the most common ones include:

i. **Procrastination**: Sometimes people can hold up everyone else in the office because they are not able to start or finish their project on time due to procrastination. They may be that person who waits until the last minute before doing anything, and, as a result, the entire office knows them as that unreliable person who cannot be trusted.

ii. **Swearing**: People do not know where to rate someone in life until they open their mouth. Perhaps these people are always speaking profanities, and, as a result, no one wants to deal with them at any given level.

iii. **Unprofessionalism**: Being unprofessional takes many forms, and it may include things such as dressing inappropriately, being a perpetual latecomer, or treating people with disrespect.

iv. **Failure to foster good relationships**: There are people who don't care about how to relate with other people because they don't think it matters. The problem is that they may end up in a difficult situation that those people could have possibly assisted them in.

v. **Poor use of time**: An employer does not pay its employees to play computer games, check on a Facebook account, or do online shopping during working hours. There are people who spend too much time surfing the net when they ought to be working. This can also cause projects to back up.

vi. **Complaining**: You have no doubt met people who always have something to complain about. They are negative about their co-workers, the government, the transport system, their friends, their family, and just about everything in their lives.

In order to overcome bad habits, we must recognize them in ourselves. It is easy to find the faults of others, but recognizing our own can be immensely difficult. Begin by taking an honest assessment of your daily life. When we examine each of the negative responses or consequences surrounding us, we should also consider the aspect of our own behavior that may have elicited these responses. It takes nothing more than this glimmer of recognition in order to begin the process of change. If you find that you habitually show up late, challenge yourself to make every effort to be early next time.

Make the effort to reach out in kindness to those around you; treat your peers as though they were your best friends. Positive energy reflects positive energy.

Eradicating addiction

Addiction refers to any self-defeating behavior that a person gets themself into and cannot possibly stop it despite any adverse consequences it has on their life. The addiction comes into the mind of the person anytime they find themselves in a crisis, under pressure, facing conflict, or compelled by boredom, and they look to the habit or substance as their way out of the situation. The problem is that looking toward the object of addiction is not a result of rational thinking. Addiction is a result of a deep-rooted response that the person may want to deny exists.

People who succumb to addiction normally spend their energy on the addictive activity because it produces a mood change in them. If you find yourself thinking about doing something in particular any time you feel hurt, bored, frightened, or angry, there is every possibility that you are addicted to that object. The ideal situation would be for you to try and admit the painful emotion you are going through and use it to pinpoint a problem you must solve.

The list of addictions is endless and can include activities, objects, or substances. Among these are: pornography, responsibility, success, work, caffeine, television, religion, relationships, the stock market, jogging and other forms of exercise, being needed, power, romance, sugar, food, shopping, sports, sex, plastic surgery, drugs, alcohol, and rage.

Dealing with addictions

No matter what addiction you might be facing, there are simple strategies that will help you in your fight to break free of it:

i. **Regain your power**: In many cases, addictions become part of our lives because of the false belief that we cannot regain control of our lives. You must determine that you have the power inside you to change, and that even if you fall back a few times, you will get up again and move on. As long as you succeed for one minute, look forward to making it for an hour, a day, a week, a month, and so on, until you regain freedom.

ii. **Look to faith**: Many people find power in a greater being for the strength to fight addictions. Religion can be a powerful tool to assist any individual to cope because it helps in the restoration of sanity.

iii.   **Commit to make a change**: This is perhaps the first step to victory, when you decide that you want to make the change that you are looking for. The life changes you are seeking should be a result of your desire to give up on the addiction.

iv.   **Take inventory**: Get out of your closet and forget about any fear, shame, or ridicule because you are not alone with addiction. There are thousands of people who have fought the same battles and have overcome. Take an inventory of your positive qualities, and then list any bad tendencies you intend to overcome; this will help your brain to assist you in the process of overcoming.

v.   **Look for help**: Realize that there are many different organizations and groups that can help you to overcome your addiction. Whether you are dealing with narcotics, alcohol, gambling, debts, or overeating, there are groups that will help you and give you all the support you require.

vi.   **Involve your family**: Your family loves you, and they probably would love to assist you in your journey out of your addiction. While you are the only one who can accomplish the task, you will find it easier if you have the support of your family members and close friends.

Letting go of "victim mentality"

Another significant way of identifying self-defeating behavior is having victim mentality. Perpetual victims are those who always feel like the world is their enemy and they don't have any control over their lives. Because such a person takes little to no action, they end up sinking in a pit of self-pity. This victim mentality offers some "benefits" that naturally attract people to feel comfortable with them. Some of these perceived benefits include:

i. **Validation of attention**: Other people normally want to attend to the victim's predicament in trying to help them out. However, this will only last for so long before people finally get tired of doing this.

ii. **No risks taken**: Since these people generally feel like a victim, they rarely venture out to do anything. As a result, they don't take any risks.

iii. **No responsibility taken**: It is hard work to take responsibility for your own life, choices and decisions. Those who believe that they are victims can make it easy on themselves momentarily because they don't have to take any responsibility.

iv. Feeling good as a victim: People who become victims can act as if everybody else must be wrong apart from them, and that can create some positive feelings.

These are some of the reasons that make it appealing to "play the victim" instead of looking for an alternative way of doing things. While it may seem like an easier way to live life, it is important to realize that we can achieve better results by being responsible and taking total control of our lives.

There are a few important strategies you can employ if you recognize that you have been feeling like a victim. Use the following techniques in your quest to give up the victim mentality:

i. **Refuse to be a victim**: Since you know the apparent benefits of being a victim, you can refuse to be associated with the emptiness of the victim mentality. Forget about blaming everything and everyone else for the things that are happening to you; forget about who has wronged you. Instead, focus on the goals you have today and how you will go about achieving them.

ii.   **Be responsible for your life**: Low self-esteem can be a byproduct of having victim mentality because you feel that you are not responsible for any aspect of your life. This type of thinking can hurt the most vital areas of your life such as your ambitions, achievements, and relationships. Accepting responsibility for your life means having power to change it.

iii.   **Attitude of gratitude**: When you get out of the victim mentality, you will finally attain a position where you will be thankful for your situation. By just becoming observant, you will realize that there are other people who have worse circumstances than you, and yet they are grateful. Allowing gratitude in our lives squelches self-pity and makes us more magnetic personalities to those around us.

iv.   **Forgiveness**: You may want to forgive different people not only for their sake but for your own good as well. Catherine Ponder once said, "When you hold resentment toward another, you are bound to that person or condition by an emotional link that is stronger than steel. Forgiveness is the only way to dissolve that link and get free." Forgiveness releases the emotional tie you have with anyone who may have wronged you.

v. **Help someone**: Try and add value to other people's lives by turning your focus away from yourself and onto other people who may be blessed by your contribution. The truth of the matter is that nature responds to the way you behave; if you are kind to people, people will be kind to you; if you show love, they will show love to you. The more you do for people, the better you will feel about you.

vi. **Take a break**: Take time to be nice to yourself even when you have slipped and failed to completely stop feeling like a victim. Remember that no one is perfect. The journey toward freedom from victimhood is not instant.

Chapter 5: Creating the path to success

We have explored how self-defeating behaviors can keep a person from accomplishing their goals in life and living up to their potential. Since it may not be very easy to recognize some of these self-sabotaging habits, taking time off to think about how we act and behave will help us a great deal. There are simple steps that you can take in order to overcome any self-defeating behavior in your life.

Recognizing weakness

The first step is the most important one, even though it may not be the easiest. This is because we may have had a habit for so many years that it becomes part and parcel of our lives. Perhaps the best thing to do would be to talk to someone you trust and to ask them about what behavior this could be in you; you may want to talk to a spouse, a friend, your parent, or a colleague.

They may be kind enough to tell you what habits they have seen in you that are a hindrance to your ability to accomplish your goals or reaching your potential. However, you must be prepared mentally not to get defensive by what you hear because you may not like what they have to say. You must also be prepared to work on it or else it will be an exercise in futility.

Replacing bad habits with positive behavior

After you have recognized the behavior that has tied you down, you must be prepared to work it out and replace it with a positive behavior. Perhaps you have had the weakness of always blaming everyone else for any problem that occurs; take it upon yourself to listen carefully next time and ask for help on how you can improve your performance with that particular issue. While this is easier said than done, you will have committed yourself to improving your life, and that will be the best opportunity to begin a life change.

Setting personal goals

Depending on what you find to be the habit you need to deal with, set a personal goal in written form and review it regularly so as to continue reminding yourself; in a little while, it will become part of your life and following through will be simply a habit.

Monitoring progress

After you have set a goal on what you plan to achieve, take time occasionally to monitor your progress. Always ask yourself why you behave the way you do, and always take stock at the end of the day on how well you performed. If you were never able to take criticism well, check how you react the next time you are criticized. If you don't react as you know you are expected to, just remind yourself that you are learning and that next time you will do better.

Remember, self-defeating habits don't form in a day, and you should therefore not expect that they will disappear overnight. Give yourself patience, and at the end of the day you will succeed.

Conclusion

You may be someone who has always had plans to make a new start in their career, marriage, or even business; at the initial stages you get excited about the prospect of becoming better but suddenly some unforeseen mental roadblocks show up, and you are unable to go on. Soon thereafter you get frustrated, and defeat follows in quick succession. For a long time, you may not have known what caused all this.

Self-defeating behavior is the enemy within-- the enemy that ignites all manner of insecurities, fears, and perceptions of failure; the enemy that prevents you from reaching those noble goals that you have always had. You don't have to feel anxious, depressed, or angry anymore, because each of these self-defeatist behaviors can be overcome. You can regain your self-confidence and drive away all the fears that have always held you back. All you need to do is to take responsibility for your life, accept your weaknesses, and work your way out of it, giving yourself sufficient time to overcome.

Be sure to visit

www.EmpowermentNation.com

to view our other books, sign up for
news, giveaways, updates, and more!

Made in the USA
Middletown, DE
31 January 2020

83859923R00042